CRYSTAL INITIATION

Guides

Atlantis: As Below So Above
A Spiritual Odyssey

Crystal Mysticism

CRYSTAL INITIATION

Lindsey Elizabeth Day

and

Keith Birch

First published in the United Kingdom in 2024 by

The Cloister House Press

ISBN 978-1-913460-85-3

Gratitude

**To all the Light Bringers,
seen and unseen, who are
helping us to prepare for
the ascension of our Race,
Thank You.**

Goods

Glimpses

All the photographs of the Crystal/Stone Light Bearers/Bringers in **CRYSTAL INITIATION** were taken by Keith Birch, the owner, along with his wife, Sandra, of KSC Crystals. They are to give you a glimpse of what the crystals look like that are mentioned in the following chapters:-

Grid

Clear Quartz Crystal Sphere
Celestite
Hematite

Growth

Agnitite
Anandalite
Apophyllite
Aragonite
Auralite 23
Azeztulite
Herkimer Diamond
Moldavite
Nirvana Quartz
Selenite
Alexandrite

Gaia's Gifts

Mani Stone

All the crystals, except Hematite, are high vibration crystals. It is important to follow the tips that are given, especially the ones **in bold**, when you are working with the high vibration crystals because the vibration of some of them can be extremely high.

The crystals that will need to be purchased for the meditation are as follows:-

> 10 Small Celestite Crystals
> 1 Clear Quartz Crystal Sphere
> 1 Hematite Stone

Gnosis

Ξ<>Ξ

We could not instantaneously see things of
which we have no recollection and that we
have never even thought of; things that we
could not invent with the imagination even
if we had plenty of time, because they are
far above our earthly understanding.....

It is impossible to overstate the value of
the riches that accompany a true
vision from God; it can even
bring health and comfort
to the physical body.

ST. TERESA OF AVILA

Greetings

The Higher Self in me greets the Higher Self in you.
When you are in the Higher Self in you,
And I am in the Higher Self in me,
We are One;
NAMESTE.

Thank you so much for joining with me for a very special spiritual journey. The combination of meditation, crystals and mantras enable the sands of time of the Material World to be parted and the World of Light, the Real World, to be entered whilst still incarnate. How deep into the World of Light you can go whilst you are meditating; what level of attunement you have to the vibration of the crystals that you are working with, and which mysteries are revealed as a result of singing the OM MANI PADME HUM mantra many times, are all according to the Grace of God. The Divine can only be reached through the subtle senses and so the way in which the Grace of God is allocated can often seem as though it is unfathomable. The overriding factor is whether your mind is open to accepting things, which can emerge whilst you are meditating, that are beyond human recognition.

The letter 'G' has been emphasized in the chapter headings as a reminder that all things are possible through the Grace of God. It truly is amazing.

Grid

When **Crystal Heaven's Magic Sphere,**
is **poised in the palm of thy fervid hand,**
thou seest enchanted shows appear

FRANCIS THOMPSON

Earth's function as a Beacon in the Cosmos is going to be fully activated again. Light Bringers, in many forms, are providing information about the Great Shift. This will be when Earth's vibration, as well as the vibration of the sentient beings on it, will be raised. By investing in a Clear Quartz Crystal Sphere, like the one below, and attuning yourself to its vibration, the sphere will help you to gain more insight into what the future will hold. (The one that I work with whilst I am meditating is very chatty.)

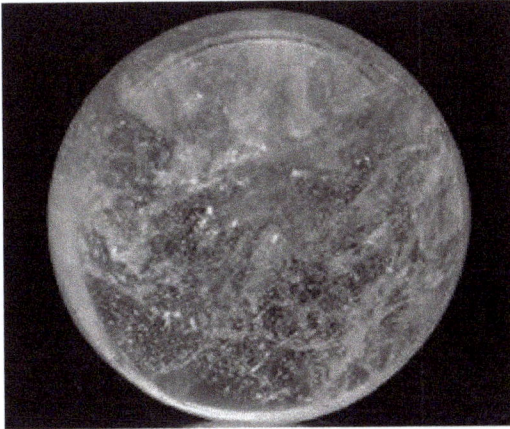

Crystal Spheres have been used for centuries to predict the future. Clear Quartz has a high vibration; it is an extremely effective transmitter, and it is associated with spiritual growth. Whilst you are shopping for the Clear Quartz Crystal Sphere, ten small blue Celestite crystals, like the one below, need to be purchased as they are going to be used to build a grid.

Placing crystals in a grid can amplify their energies and setting out the Celestite Grid on your meditation table, first of all, will help you to maintain the focus of the Initiation whilst you are in the meditative state. The Grid is associated with Grace and Growth, and it is called the 'Arrow of Ascension.' The arrowhead points towards the higher realm that will be reached with the assistance of various Light Bringers. Celestite is particularly well known for facilitating a connection being made with members of the Angelic Hierarchy and one of them will be your Guardian throughout the whole of the meditation.

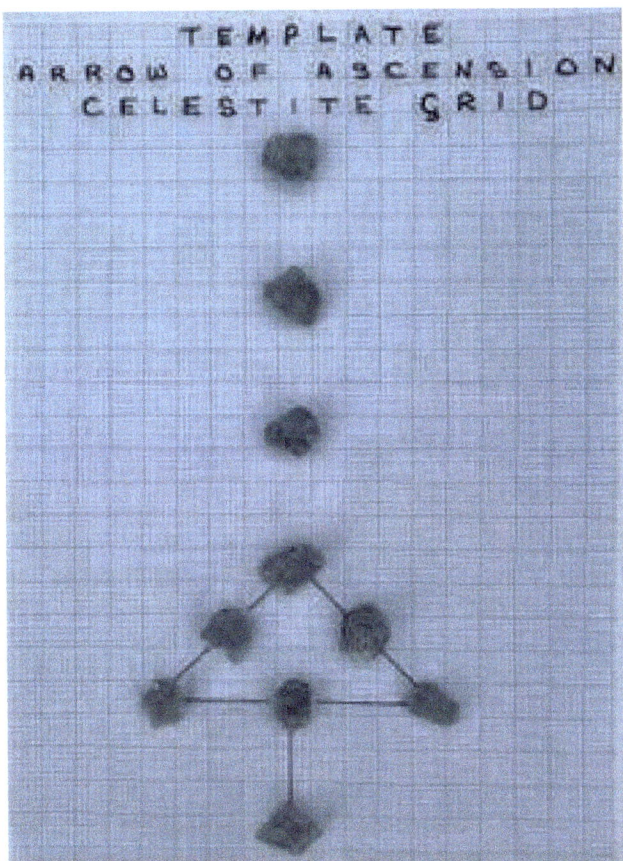

TEMPLATE
ARROW OF ASCENSION
CELESTITE GRID

To attune myself to the vibration/properties of individual crystals, I brush each one of them with a soft little brush that is kept solely for use on crystals. Brushing them not only removes dust from the stones, it can also strengthen the bond made with the crystals as they seem to enjoy being gently brushed. Next, I hold the stone against my Heart Chakra; thank God for the gift of the crystal and ask that it is cleansed and purified by pure white light. I envisage a stream of white light coming down from high above me and watch as this light passes through the whole of the stone. Finally, I ask if there is anything that the crystal wants to convey to me.

An excellent tip of Keith's is to hold a Hematite stone, like the one on the next page, when working with high vibration crystals. Hematite has an earthy vibration, and it can combat any nausea or feelings of being ungrounded or spaced out that can occur until you are acclimatized to the frequency that the crystals vibrate on.

Hematite's reputation of being the best stone for grounding as well as being a very good stone of protection is well deserved. Another of its attributes is that it is a calming stone that can assist in bringing anxiety under control, which is not only beneficial for your health, it can also help you if the thought scares you of entering a state of consciousness that is higher than you have accessed before.

HEMATITE

Before you set the Celestite crystals out on your table, make sure that they will not be sitting in direct sunlight as their lovely blue colour will fade. In addition, they need to be handled carefully as they are very soft and can easily be damaged.

You need to programme every one of the ten Celestite crystals. Ask that all their good energies are activated for your benefit and then specify your intention for using each crystal, which is to help and support you through the Initiation. (The Clear Quartz Sphere and the Hematite stone are programmed in the same way.)

Six of the Celestite crystals are laid out, from the bottom of your meditation table to the top of it, in a straight vertical line with a small gap between each stone. One of the remaining stones is placed on the left side of the second stone up from the bottom of the grid with a small gap between them. The other stone is put on the right side of this crystal, also with a small gap between them, so a straight horizontal line is formed. The two remaining stones are part of the arrowhead and are placed on the table as shown on the diagram that is on the next page.

The energy of Celestite crystals is gentle and calming and feelings of joy and bliss can arise from working with these stones. This is due to their high vibration.

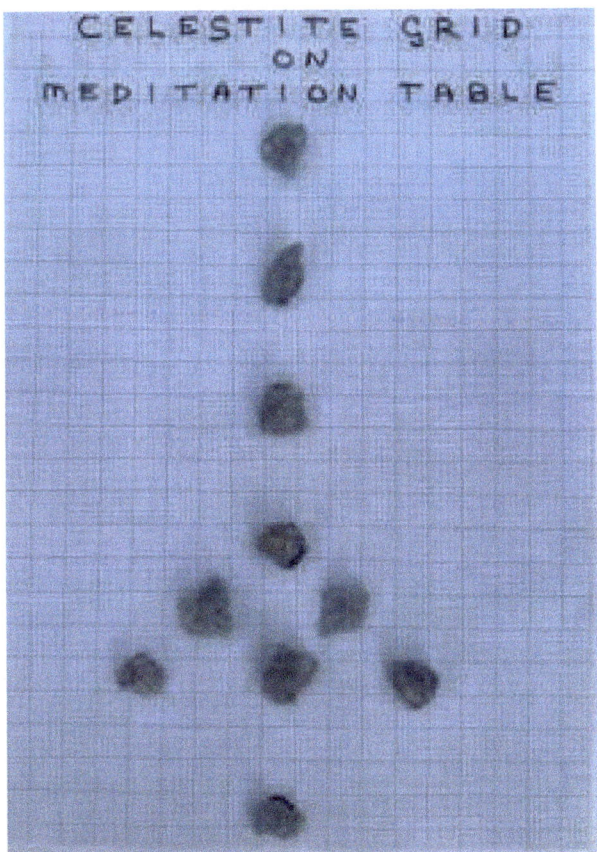

CELESTITE GRID
ON
MEDITATION TABLE

By investing in high vibration crystals, the growth of your spiritual wealth can increase in an extraordinary way. Spiritual wealth brings constant contentment, happiness, ever-new bliss and deep peace, and the benefits do not end there either. When you obtain the State of Grace that enables you to accumulate the riches that are valued in the World of Light, what is revealed to you about the World of Light remains with you not only for this lifetime; it can be brought to the surface again in other lifetimes because consciousness never dies.

The level of serenity that can come from working with Celestite crystals is vital for the deeper meditative state that is needed for the Initiation. This is because the Initiation that is going to take place into the powers of high vibration crystals will entail information of a profound nature being brought to light.

There is a garden in the world that is parallel to the one in which you think you dwell. It is where all the mysteries originate. Although there has been much debate, about the mysterious garden, unless you are in a deep meditative state, you are unlikely to succeed in understanding where it is located.

Provided that all your efforts to gain entry to the garden are genuinely heartfelt, confirmation that your request for permission to go into the garden has been approved will be obtained by the exquisite perfume of The Rose being smelt. You will then be freed from the limitations of the human mind and able to assimilate guidance from Light Bringers who are usually unseen.

The kiss on your brow of The Sun/Son's Golden Light will, through God's Grace, enable things to appear that will raise your consciousness to a new height. Not only will you view the way in which the new dawn of our divinity will be defined, the manner in which it will be outlined will cause a level of enlightenment to unfold that will be a very precious gift to hold.

Make sure that you keep both of your feet on the floor whilst you are meditating and that you hold the Hematite stone throughout the meditation to ground the knowledge in yourself that you will be receiving. If possible, sit on a dining room chair during the meditation on the Initiation as it will help you to keep your back straight.

Light a white tealight or candle. Then place your left hand horizontally over your Heart Chakra and your right hand on top of your left hand. Keep your arms horizontal and your fingers straight. Raise your thumbs as high as they will go and put the pads of your thumbs together. An upward pointing triangle is made above the area of your Heart Chakra by doing this. It symbolizes transcendence. With your inner voice, say:-

I am protected and blessed by the Divine Light of Spiritual Protection which flows through my whole being and surrounds my whole being at all times.

Breathe in to the count of three and feel your abdomen rise. Hold your breath for the count of three. Breathe out to the count of three feeling your abdomen contract. Hold your breath for the count of three. Do this whole exercise three times. It will help the divine energy, which is stored in the Base/Root Chakra, to rise up your central light column to your Heart Chakra.

The Heart Chakra is the bridge between the lower chakras associated with our human nature and the higher chakras connected with our divine nature. The Grid illuminates the course that the meditation will take. The crystal that is placed at the bottom of your meditation table relates to the Heart Chakra. The Initiation starts from there because of the level of Ascended Heart Consciousness that needs to be opened up in order for knowledge to be gained about a very high chakra.

Pick up the Hematite stone and the Clear Quartz sphere and as you gaze into the sphere start singing, with your inner voice, the following Tibetan mantra,

OM MANI PADME HUM

It has been chanted by initiates through the centuries to help them not only gain a higher state of spiritual awakening; but also because they believe that the consciousness of humanity is raised at the same time. Although the mantra has been translated as,

The Jewel of Consciousness
is in the Heart Chakra

to be effective, the translation of the mantra should not be sung, only the holy words of sacred mantras are expressed. This is because it is not possible to translate into earthly languages all the levels of meaning of the holy words. The holy words of this mantra are pronounced as follows:-

om mah-nee pahd-mey hoom

As you are repeating the mantra, you become aware that a very tall Being is with you. His appearance elicits a feeling of awe and when he asks you if you are ready to take part in the Initiation, you ask him if he is from The Light. He replies, "I am." You ask him again if he is from The Light. He replies, "I am." You ask him a third time if he is from The Light. He replies, "I am. My name is Archangel Metatron." He asks you again if you are ready to take part in the Initiation. You confirm that you are ready, and Metatron says, "So be it."

Guardians

The Angels keep their ancient places;
Turn but a stone and start a wing.

FRANCIS THOMPSON

Human Beings have been designed so that they can accommodate an expansion of consciousness of the higher dimensions of the World of Light. Throughout the meditation on the Initiation you will be protected by many seen and unseen Guardians.

Archangel Metatron will be your Guardian throughout the meditation and he will be overseeing Grade I of the Initiation. He is known as 'the Elect One.' During his life on Earth he was called, 'Enoch.' Enoch 'Walked with God,' listened to SHI (God) and his heart was on fire with the Love of SHI. He was taken up to the Throne of Glory in a fiery chariot. Metatron is, therefore, the ideal Guardian to start the process that will eventually entail knowledge being opened up to you about the re-configuration of the Tree of Life. The power and purity of the light that comes from the Archangel reflects spiritual growth of the magnitude that will be required for Human Beings' continued existence on Earth. As he gazes at you, your Guardian gently says, "Peace be with you, Beloved Child of The Light, there is nothing to fear about being enfolded in my light. Take your awareness to the Sacred Heart Chakra now, for that is where Grade I of the Initiation occurs."

GRADE I

God's Gifts

If I have the gift of prophecy and understand
all mysteries and all knowledge...
but have not love, I am nothing.

1 CORINTHIANS 13:2

Metatron informs you that God's Garden vibrates on a high frequency and in order to enter the Garden, you need to know SHI's Name. He tells you that he will be teaching you how to sing God's Name in the Cherishing Language. The Archangel makes you aware that the chamber that you are in has a very important bearing on whether you will be admitted to the Garden. This is because SHI's Name not only has to be pronounced correctly, it also has to be expressed with love and pure consciousness.

The Chamber of Purification

Metatron turns on a shower of white light and when the purification process has been completed, he puts a long white garment on you. On a pocket that is over your Heart Chakra, there is an image of a red rose, a white rose and a gold rose, one above the other. Before putting a Holy Stone in the pocket, the Archangel shows you the symbol that is engraved on the stone. It consists of an arrow with four circles above the arrowhead. A vertical zigzag, which is the symbol of a Lightning Strike, is entering the highest circle. Once he has put the stone in the pocket of the gown, Metatron tells you that you can now go into the second chamber.

The Chamber of Resonance

As soon as you are in the chamber, your Guardian starts singing the letters of the Name of SHI in a rhythm that is something like a fairly fast heartbeat.

l-l-l mmmmmmm roo-oo-oo-oo-shhh-shhh-shhh inggg-inggg-inggg Ahhh/ k-tahhh-ahhh-ahhh zzzer–er-er Ahhh/ shoo-oo-oo-oo-shhh-shhh-shhh Ahhh

The Archangel explains that the Jewel of Consciousness in the Heart Chakra has many facets. Each facet is included in the Name of SHI and after each facet SHI's Love is expressed as the sound of 'Ahhh.' He says that although you will only be learning the shorter version of The Name, at a later stage he will be revealing some more letters of The Name to you.

Metatron then explains that the letters **l m roo sh ing** reflect the Mighty Presence of SHI; the letters **k ta zer** relate to the Great Soul of SHI, and the letters **sh oo sh** refer to the Great Spirit of SHI. He makes you aware that you have to keep repeating The Name, like a mantra, in the same rhythm that he used, until you have mastered how to express the letters of The Name perfectly. It takes you a long time, and a lot of tuition, before the Archangel confirms that you are sounding the first part of The Name with the correct level of intonation and heartfelt expression and that you are ready to go into the next chamber. He informs you that he will reveal the letters of

The Name that illuminate The Light of SHI to you once you are in there.

The Chamber of Light

The lesson begins with your Guardian singing the next letters of The Name in the same rhythm as the first part of The Name. They are:-

Si-i-i sa-a-a L Ahhh/ mw br rrr–rrr-rrr zzz Ahhh/ fw zzz zer-er-er Ahhh/ i-i-i-i L ee-ee-ee shhh-shhh-shhh Ahhh/ w-w-w j-j-j l-l-l Ahhh/ wm dd-dd-dd der-er-er ree-ee-een Ahhh

Metatron advises you that the letters **si sa L/ mw br r z/ fw z zer** all relate to The Light that is emitted from the Spirit of SHI, the Great Central Sun, **si sa L**. He remarks that it has been said that if a thousand suns appeared simultaneously in the sky, their light might dimly resemble the splendour of The Light of SHI's Spirit. Then he tells you that the letters **mw br r z,** refer to the Fire of the Spirit of SHI. It is a ray from the Great Central Sun that has been likened to a Lightning Strike; whereas the power of the Spirit of SHI's Light, **fw z zer** has been described as being like a tornado, for it lifts you up and carries you to a higher place.

Next, your Guardian tells you that the letters **i L ee sh** refer to the radiance of The Light that is emitted from the Soul of SHI and that the radiance has been likened to the light of the moon; the letters **w j l** reflect the profound power of SHI's Love, and the letters **wm dd der reen** relate to the perfect peace of SHI. Metatron adds that using the terms 'Sun' and 'Moon' are so that there is some semblance of understanding of the Light emitted from SHI's Spirit and Soul as, at present, it is beyond the understanding of Human Beings. The Archangel assures you that the power of The Name has been stepped down so that you are protected whilst you are expressing The Name. He says this will not stop you from receiving blessings and gifts from SHI.

You diligently practise repeating the letters that you have just been made aware of numerous times until Metatron approves of the way that you are expressing them. Then you have to sing, very many times, all of the letters of The Name that have been revealed to you before the Archangel informs you that whilst you were singing the Name of SHI, the love and peace radiating from your human soul demonstrated how far you have come up the Ladder of Ascending Heart Consciousness. He says this means that you are ready to try and gain entry to a very special chamber.

The Chamber of The Presence

When you arrive at the door of the fourth chamber, your Guardian informs you that SHI listens to all the petitions that are made by an Initiate when they enter the chamber where the Presence of SHI can be found. Apart from expressing the whole of the shorter version of The Name of God correctly when SHI is asked to grant a divine privilege, the flame of Divine Love, in the heart of the Initiate, has to be burning brightly and constantly when the petition is presented. It indicates that they are ready to receive what they have asked for. They will not be given the blessings or gift that they most desire if these conditions are not met.

Metatron asks you what you think the mantra is that opens the door. The answer comes from deep within your heart and you say, "I Am because I Am Love."

The Archangel responds by saying, "How deep is this Love?" You reply, "Love is all."

Metatron says again, "How deep is this Love?" Due to the level of understanding that you have gained of Divine Love, you are able to bring more power to your response and you reply, "Love is all, Love is all."

The Archangel says again, "How deep is this Love?" With great depth of feeling, you reply, "Love is all, Love is all, Love is ALL, OM MANI PADME HUM."

The door opens signifying that "the words of your mouth and the meditation of your heart are acceptable" and as soon as you go into the chamber, you are immediately aware of the Presence of SHI.

A wonderful feeling of peace comes over you as you realize that, without a shadow of doubt, you are loved beyond measure. Knowing how much you are loved, you are able to calmly sing SHI's Name. With due reverence, you raise your arms above your head, with your hands in prayer position, when you express **'L,' 'fw'** and the final **'Ahhh,'** before stating your case. You say:-

"I-I-I mmmmmmm roo-oo-oo-oo-shhh-shhh-shhh inggg-inggg-inggg Ahhh, k-tahhh-ahhh-ahhh zzzer-er-er Ahhh, shoo-oo-oo-oo-shhh-shhh-shhh Ahhh, si-i-i sa-a-a L^ Ahhh, mw br rrr-rrr-rrr zzz Ahhh, **fw**^ zzz zer-er-er Ahhh, i-i-i **L**^ ee-ee-ee shhh-shhh-shhh Ahhh, w-w-w j-j-j I-I-I Ahhh, wm dd-dd-dd der-er-er ree-ee-een **Ahhh**^,[1] I am aware that great events take place in the parallel world before they are made manifest on the physical plane. May I enter Your Garden so that I can find out more about the Great Event that is on the horizon for the Human Race? I humbly ask that you grant me the Gift of Prophesy so that I can share the information that I obtain with those who also want to be as prepared as possible for the re-configuration of the Tree of Life and what it will entail." You put your hands in prayer position against your Heart Chakra and say, "Glory," then you move your hands to your Third Eye Chakra and say, "be to," back again to your Heart Chakra and say, "God," and then bow your head. There is complete silence for what seems like a very long time. Suddenly, the Holy Stone starts vibrating in the pocket of your garment and a powerful jolt goes through the whole of your being as a wondrous vision of The Rose emerges. The white light that is being emitted from The Rose is so pure, so sacred, and so sublime that you are mesmerized by its beauty; the exquisite fragrance of SHI fills the chamber, and a feeling of absolute joy comes over you; for it means that you have been granted the divine privilege that you asked for and, in addition, you have been blessed by having direct experience of SHI.

---

[1]Information about the correct pronunciation of the letters of The Name can be found in the chapter called, 'Growth.'

You put your hands in prayer position against your Heart Chakra and say, with deep respect and love, "Beloved God, Your Name, Your Works, and Your Love are glorious in my sight."

Metatron gives you a big hug and says, "Dear One, you are indeed blessed. The Great Soul of SHI is revealed in myriad guises. They are witnessed according to the level of Ascended Heart Consciousness that has awakened in you. To see the Almighty One, in the guise of the White Rose, signifies that a very special Teacher is waiting for you in the Garden. He was once mistaken as being a gardener.[1] He is, however, a High Priest of The Order of Melchizedek. It is an eternal Priesthood and as a result, he is very qualified to make you aware of what you need to know. Bask in the love and the light that will flow to you from him. It will help you to assimilate what will be revealed to you about the Glory of God's Grace once Grade II of the Initiation is completed. I will be here when it is time for you to return to the Inner, Inner Sanctum of the Sacred Heart Centre." With that, the Archangel guides you to where the gate of the mysterious garden is located, in the Realm of the Sacred Heart, and opens the gate for you.

[1] Gospel of St. John 20:15

GRADE

II

God's Garden

**The Glory of the Garden
lies in more than meets the eye.**

RUDYARD KIPLING

You notice, as your Teacher approaches you, that he is wearing a long white garment. There is an image of the Great Central Sun, with a gold rose in the centre of it, over his Heart Chakra. The High Priest's arms are open wide, and the warmth of his greeting fills your heart with joy. He places the sacred kiss on your brow and a vision of the Garden's Conservatory emerges. It looks like a gold palace because a ray from the Great Central Sun is shining on the Conservatory. Your Teacher tells you that the Initiation is going to continue in the Conservatory. He says that The Powers that you once had, and the knowledge that you once knew about some of The Mysteries are going to be retrieved.

The Conservatory

As soon as the High Priest takes you into the Conservatory, the High Priestess, who is called, Mary, comes forward and gives you a big hug. She says, "Welcome to the Sisterhood and Brotherhood of The Rose. It is the community of those who actually know God instead of merely knowing about God. This is because the Name of God has been revealed to them and so they know SHI to a greater extent than is normal in those who are incarnate."

On the front of the Priestess' headgear there is a red rose, a white rose and a gold rose, one above the other. She tells you that the red rose represents SHI's Heart. Next, Mary explains that the white rose is the surrogate for SHI's 'Face.' Not only is SHI's Face seen when SHI's Name is known; awareness of the power, as well as the purity and radiance of SHI's Light is obtained and from then on God begins to really be known. Then the High Priestess makes you aware that the gold rose exemplifies SHI's Infinite Mind, which contains the gold light of wisdom; wisdom that is far greater than all the wisdom possessed by all who are wise.

Mary informs you that she is going to help you to remember how to express the names of seven Powers of The Light first of all. She says that these powers will accelerate your progress. You will be able to call on each one individually or one after the other if it is deemed to be necessary. The High Priestess explains that by singing the names in the Cherishing Language, their potency is enhanced, and that each name of the Power of The Light is followed by 'Ahhh,' which is sung very lovingly, from your heart, like an echo of the outpouring of the warmth of the expression of SHI's Love. You learn that, as with a mantra, all the names have to be expressed correctly and sung over and over before each power is properly activated and that as you express them, the sound of your voice should be joyful and harmonious.

The name of the 1st Power of The Light is **Dagerdu Ahhh.** Mary says that it is associated with Clairvoyance, which is the power to see with the Third Eye in the brow, or with the Eye of the Heart, an event from the past; one that is happening in the present, or one that is going to take place in the future. They will be witnessed on one of the higher planes that are beyond space and time

Once you have perfected the art of singing the name of the 1st Power, the High Priestess tells you that you are ready to start singing the name of the 2nd Power, which is **Weezonfat Ahhh**. She reveals that it is related to Clairaudience. This is the ability to hear sounds, music and voices that cannot be heard on the normal auditory range. After Mary has sung the name to you, you keep repeating it until she starts singing the name of the 3rd Power.

The name of the 3rd Power of The Light is **Buseenet Ahhh**. The High Priestess explains that this power is similar to Clairsentience, which is the ability to obtain information through intuition. One way, in human terms, is through having a gut feeling about something. Mary smiles when you tell her that you have experienced a gut feeling that you have mastered the pronunciation of the name of the 3rd Power and that you are ready for her to sing the name of the next power to you.

After the High Priestess has sung the name of the 4th Power of The Light, which is **Pagrodisvu Ahhh**, she tells you that this power is the power of Clairmonstrance. It is on a higher frequency than Clairsentience and it is the ability to specifically recognize the level of divinity or holiness in a vessel of any kind and act accordingly.

When you have practised singing the 4th Power, Mary sings the name of the 5th Power of The Light in a way that causes the sound of her voice to keep on echoing in your Heart Chakra. Its name, in The Cherishing Language is **Pepertan Ahhh**. The High Priestess reminds you that this power concerns Clairresonance. It can be likened to Telepathy except that it is heart-to-heart communication not mind-to-mind transmission. It is, therefore, a more sacred power than Telepathy.

As soon as you are ready to go on to the next power, Mary informs you that the 6th Power is Clairobservance. It is the ability to discern the ways of The Divine and accept them with great reverence and true appreciation of them. This occurs because the level of your attunement to The Light has been heightened by the activation of this power as it enables the level of spiritual evolvement that was achieved in your past lives to be observed. You are able to remember how to sing the name of the sixth power, which is **Moleevu Ahhh**, without any difficulty.

Before the High Priestess sings the name of the 7th Power of The Light to you, she explains that it is aligned with Claircognisance. It relates to knowledge of Divine Mysteries. Mary says that the divine knowing that is associated with the activation of the 7th Power, which is called **Paseeranusveech Ahhh**, is at a higher evolved level, though, because it is only activated when the Name of SHI is known. Once you have perfected your expression of the name of the 7th Power, the High Priestess reminds you of the names of the five Mysteries of The World of Light that you once knew:-

YImozemfaktor Ahhh is the Mystery of the Guerdon of Grace. Its allocation can seem unfathomable unless the 6th Power has been obtained.

Isneemuspouvareen Ahhh is the Mystery of the Magnetism of The Rose. It attracts those who are inspired to achieve great works for SHI.

Husgerveenerbedeesem Ahhh is the Mystery of The Return. The key to understanding it is that it is the Will of SHI that it takes place.

Mozenbikdeela Ahhh is the Mystery of the Burning Bush. It signifies that the next level of the evolution of Humankind is about to be brought into being.

FeeveroL^tu Ahhh is the Mystery of The Name of SHI. When God says I AM ....., a dramatic profound change takes place.

When you know the names of the seven Powers of The Light off by heart again, as well as the names of the five Mysteries of The Light, the High Priestess asks you to sing the names one after the other. Once you have finished singing **Dagerdu Ahhh, Weezonfat Ahhh, Buseenet Ahhh, Pagrodisvu Ahhh, Pepertan Ahhh, Moleevu Ahhh, Paseeranusveech Ahhh, YImozemfaktor Ahhh, Isneemuspouvareen Ahhh, Husgerveenerbedeesem Ahhh, Mozenbikdeela Ahhh, FeeveroL^tu Ahhh,**[1]

[1]Pronunciation of the names of The Powers and The Mysteries can be found in the chapter called, 'Growth.'

Mary gives you a very tender loving hug before placing a special Crystal Sphere in your hand. You experience a lovely sensation of a warm glow spreading throughout your Heart Chakra and you realize that the crystal has an extremely high vibration.

The High Priestess tells you that the power of the light that is being emitted from the sphere will not harm you in any way. Your consciousness has been tuned, by singing the names of The Powers and The Mysteries, to higher frequencies than you would have been able to tolerate before you began the Initiation. She informs you that in order for the sphere to help you to gain a deeper level of awareness of The Mysteries, you need to hold it against your Heart Chakra so that all the images that emerge are seen with the Eye of the Heart.

At first you can only see silver, gold and white light in the sphere. Suddenly, though, letters, numbers and symbols emerge. They are rapidly computed, and the calculation produces an image of a magnificent fountain. Within the centre of the fountain's sparkling light you are able to see The Rose. A vast lush green lawn then materializes, and your heart starts singing with joy; for it means that the Garden of SHI has been fully opened up to you because you will now be able to tolerate the power of the light that is in the Garden.

The Observatory

The High Priest tells you that the Being who is coming towards you across the lawn is the Light Bringer, St. John The Divine. You recall that his symbol as a Gospel writer was the eagle and that another book attributed to him was called, 'The Revelation of St. John The Divine.' The image that you see of John is as he was when he was about thirty years old. He has curly chestnut coloured hair, a short curly beard and warm, twinkling eyes. John greets you like a long-lost friend, and then he tells you that he is going to take you to the Observatory so that you can see what is on the horizon for Humankind. On the way to this building, you pass an amazing Rockery. Crystals and gemstones of every sort that are found in the Universe are laid out in a glorious array.

The Observatory is circular. Its white framework houses, what looks like, numerous panes of glass. As you enter the building you see that there is a huge Crystal Sphere in the centre of the Observatory. It seems to be suspended in mid-air. John makes you aware that the sphere is controlled by voice and gaze. You stare at the sphere as you sing the 1st Power of The Light, **Dagerdu Ahhh**.

The sphere begins rotating and you are able to see that it is balanced on a gyroscope. An image, which relates to the future, rapidly emerges. It is of Al-Haram As-Sharif/Har HaBayit/the Dome of the Rock, in Jerusalem. It is being destroyed by a seismic event, as foretold[1] and you are filled with an intense feeling of fear; for you are then able witness what happens next.

[1]P.17 Crystal Mysticism

John says, "The plane of Armageddon, on which the Great Battle will take place, has been marked out precisely. A catastrophe of this magnitude will be very hard to bear in human terms. Any words used to describe such an occurrence are totally inadequate; but because you have seen this image, you will be prepared for what is going to happen.

"Abide in faith that help will be provided and the next step up the ladder of evolution will occur. The Great Shift is going to be brought into being because the evil in the Material World is reaching epic proportions. Arch-rivals will compete to do the greatest damage; but they will not succeed. The darkness in them will not be able to tolerate the glorious arrays of the power and radiance of God's Light that will emerge.

"The delay in the emergence of the New World is because of the intransigence of the Human Race in general. The best that they could manage was not good enough for what was lost a long time ago to be regained. The only way to overcome this is for the re-configuration of the Human Being so 'The Return' can take place. You will learn more about it shortly. Know, with absolute certainty that all that is going to pass away is going to be replaced with something better because it is ready for renewal. What is on the horizon for Humankind is what many have been seeking but were not able to find."

John alters the tilt of the sphere and says, "Praises to you, Dear One, for the path that you are on has accelerated your journey up the Ladder of Ascending Heart Consciousness and you have been invited to a feast. During it you will see the Tree of Life being re-configured. Each piece of information that you will be given is so that a wider level of understanding is gained about the Great Shift in Human Beings. The Human Race is going to be given the chance to rise again to its former glory. Its passport to greater understanding of The Light will be knowledge of the Name of SHI."

Before you leave the Observatory, an image appears in the sphere of another future event. The area where Al-Haram As-Sharif/Har HaBayit/the Dome of the Rock once stood is being re-consecrated by the High Priest and Priestess in readiness for the replacement of the old building.

Feast of the Fire of Great Spirit

John takes you to a large white marquee that is filled with many Beings of Light. Some of them you have met before, such as Melchezidek; others have been unseen until now, and there are those whose presence you are aware of; but you are not able to see them because their vibration is on a frequency that you are not fully able to tune into yet.

A Precious One of Very High Standing comes forward with the High Priest and Priestess. The love and compassion in her eyes as she gazes at you makes you feel incredibly moved and honoured by her presence at your Initiation. The sound of the voice of the High Priest's Mother, as she greets you, reminds you of the gentle cooing of a dove. She says, "Gracious One, the sustenance that you will partake will enable your voice to flow like honey when you tell your earthly companions about this magnificent feast."

The feast begins with everyone looking at the centre of the lawn, for it is where the Tree of Life stands. You watch as a tall branch is grafted back on to the Tree so that the Ultimate Expression of the Human Race can come into being again. The High Priest blesses the next step that you are about to take up the Ladder of Ascending Heart Consciousness and then Mary guides you to a lawn that is located at a higher level.

On the lawn there is a 'bed' of white rose petals. The Priestess helps you to lie down on the bed and then she and the High Priest and his Mother stand round the bed with the Archangels and their partners who you saw in the marquee. Constance and Metatron, who is the 'Keeper of the Watch,' are at the foot of the bed. Joy and Barachiel, who is associated with the White Rose and whose name means, 'God's Blessings,' are on the opposite side of the bed to the High Priest's Mother. Clarity and Jophiel, whose name means, 'God's Beauty,' are opposite the High Priestess. Faith and Michael, whose name means, 'God's Shadow' (One who is like God), are opposite the High Priest. Hope and Gabriel, whose name means, 'God's Strength,' are opposite St. John The Divine. Victory and Raziel, whose name means, 'God's Secrets/Mysteries,' are opposite Melchizedek. Next to Melchizedek are Radiance and Haniel, whose name means, 'God's Glory.' Opposite Radiance and Haniel are Freedom and Jeremiel, whose name means, 'God's Mercy.' Next to Freedom and Jeremiel are Purity and Zadkiel, whose name means, 'God's Righteousness.' At the top of the bed are Uriel, whose name means, 'God's Light' and Brigid, the goddess called, 'The Midwife.' She is assisting with the birthing of greater understanding of the Fire of SHI.

Whilst you are lying on the bed, a vision emerges of all those who were round the bed accompanying you as you go into an arbour that is covered with white rose petals. At the end of the arbour there is a burning bush. Summoning up all your courage, you slowly make your way towards the bush; but once you are standing in front of the burning bush of The Rose, the sublime fragrance coming from the bush elicits a wonderful feeling of calmness and serenity. As a result, you are able to grasp that your companions are with you to protect you as you complete Grade II of the Initiation, and that the flames have been cast out of the Perfect Love of SHI. Your fear of what might be going to happen next completely disappears. Indeed, you feel no pain as the flames burn away the things that are no longer needed and purify your being so that you can experience what the transfiguration of the human self is going to entail.

Suddenly, the crackling noise of the flames stops. The silence that follows is eerie. Time, as you know it, seems to stand still. In SHI's own time, your heart is filled with the sound of the Almighty One's Voice. Its power causes your whole being to shake; your heart feels as though it is on fire with SHI's Love, and yet you can clearly hear God say:-

"I-I-I mmmmmmm roo-oo-oo-oo-shhh-shhh-shhh inggg-inggg-inggg Ahhh, k-tahhh-ahhh-ahhh zzzer-er-er Ahhh, shoo-oo-oo-oo-shhh-shhh-shhh Ahhh, si-i-i sa-a-a L Ahhh, mw br rrr-rrr-rrr zzz Ahhh, fw zzz zer-er-er Ahhh, i-i-i L ee-ee-ee shhh-shhh-shhh Ahhh, w-w-w j-j-j l-l-l Ahhh, wm dd-dd-dd der-er-er ree-ee-een Ahhh. Rejoice in the raising of the veil. The Glory of My Grace awaits you."

Numerous red sparks explode from the rose bush in a magnificent display of the power of the Eternal Flame of SHI's Love; Uriel and Brigid open the very special gold gates of the Stellar Gateway; the vivid zigzag of a Lightning Strike flashes before you; you are instantly taken up to a higher level, and something that has been hidden for very long time is revealed to you.

GRADE III

God's Grace

Grace is the spirit, which came out of the Height through the First Mystery, who had mercy on humanity. Through this spirit they are able to receive The Mysteries and inherit the Kingdom of Light.

PISTIS SOPHIA I.61

Standing behind the Throne of Glory, which is in the God Chakra, is Archangel Michael; for as it is written, "S/he who dwells in the secret place of the Most High shall abide under the Shadow of the Almighty."[1] The High Priest and High Priestess are on either side of the Throne. It is made of white crystal and on the Throne, there is a Clear Quartz Crystal Skull that has a hole in the top of the skull. The High Priest picks up the skull and invites you to sit on the throne. Its purity is so obvious that you feel unworthy and even afraid to do so. Your Teacher tells you there was the level of assimilation of God's Name for the God Chakra to be unveiled to you; there is nothing to fear, for it is the Wheel of Celestial Joy, and that the river of light that flows from its Throne enables many gates to be opened in the Realm of Celestial Joy.

[1] Psalm 91:1

Once you are sitting on the Throne, the High Priest holds the skull in front of you. He tells you that it was crafted in Atlantis, and it signifies the return of a more crystalline brain in the Human Being as it was in the Golden Age of Atlantis. Your Teacher breathes into the hole in the top of the skull; eyes that are deep in the sockets are opened; white light is emitted from the eyes, ears, nose and mouth, and the jaw starts moving. A noise is emitted from the mouth that sounds like a huge sigh of relief that the knowledge stored in the skull during Atlantean times can now be released. Only one word is transmitted to you. The word is 'Peace.'

The High Priest says, "History repeats itself so learnedness can be gained at a higher level; mistakes can be rectified, and a new way forward can be achieved. Human consciousness has nearly completed a trek of epic proportions. It has been undertaken in preparation for the monumental journey into divine consciousness that the Human Race will be embarking upon very soon. A total explanation has not been possible of the Mysteries of The Light that you are aware of because there is not the capacity to receive this knowledge yet. Adjustments are already being made to remedy this. As more crystals are activated in the pineal gland, more light is entering, and being emitted from, Human Light Bringers." He tells you that other changes, regarding the Great Event of the upgrading of the Human Being, are going to be opened up to you now so that a higher perspective of the future encasement of the soul in a human body is gained.

Your Teacher comments that there has been much debate about the reasons for the encasement of the soul in a human body, but a satisfactory conclusion has not been obtained of why this particular model was devised. It cannot be used in other locations giving the impression, to some, that humans are the only beings existing in the Universe. He says, "As soon as Earth Beings are able to fully understand the intricacies of Creation, there will be nothing that cannot be achieved by the Human Race. Light is already filtering through at a higher frequency and progress is being made. Greater understanding of the presence of Extraterrestrials is now starting to be gained and pathways will be opened up so that knowledge can be obtained about all of the other beings that dwell in the Universe. Beyond that Human Beings will not be able to go, but their spirits will."

The High Priestess puts a skull cap on your head that consists of ten pockets. She explains that in the pockets there are ten crystals that she has gathered from the Rockery in God's Garden and informs you that the crystals in the cap will help you attune to what you are going to be finding out during Grade III of the Initiation. Next, the High Priestess puts a gold heart shaped amulet round your neck and tells you that it is to protect you whilst you are being made aware of the transfiguration process. She reveals that the amulet contains the Name of SHI and a very small piece of the Tantermani Fiery Stone.[1] Mary says that this crystal will assist in tolerance being gained to the higher frequency vibration that you will be experiencing in your being.

[1] P.84, Crystal Mysticism

The High Priestess tells you that one of the miraculous changes that will take place is the level of the depth of God's Love for Creation that will be opened up in humans. It will demonstrate the ascension of our heart consciousness and the expansion of our divine nature. With love and wisdom, we will reach out to others regardless of their ethnicity, creeds, previous hostilities, and so on, in a way that will seem alien to many of those on Earth at present.

The High Priest puts three drops of Holy Oil on your Heart Chakra signifying that the process is about to begin for the In-Fusion of God's Grace that you are going to receive. Your Teacher directs a ray from the Great Central Sun into your Soul Chakra and tells you that your Light Body is being prepared for the In-Fusion. Colourless liquid then starts flowing through it and he informs you that it is called, 'Divine Plasma.' The High Priest tells you that it contains the next level of exemplary particles and that they will bring about:-

1.   The updating of the filament in the Light-body of humans. This will be connected to the vibration of humans being on a higher frequency. Higher voltage Lightning Strikes will be able to be tolerated as a consequence.

2.   The level of Ascended Heart Consciousness where humans will be able to absorb the level of SHI's Wisdom that the Beings called 'The Immortals' have obtained.

3.   An increase in the pulse of humans. This is so that it is aligned with the rhythm of the pulse in the Immortals.

4.   The emergence of a more godlike nature. It will involve the attributes of the Holy Self being activated to a higher degree and the flow of pure consciousness increasing.

Your Teacher says that the effect of the exemplary particles will be as though a light bulb has been switched on. More light, in the form of knowledge, will be able to enter humans and darkness, in the form of ignorance, will be removed. They will be able to wholeheartedly accept the change in reality that will result from the raising of the frequency on which Human Beings vibrate, and the whole of the Human Race will no longer have the inclination to go to war.

Finally, the High Priest directs a Lightning Strike into the right side of your chest. He informs you that now that the exemplary particles are within you and a spark from the Fire of the Spirit of SHI is in your soul, the activation of a new heart in you, and in all Human Beings, will begin on the Great Day when the New Dawn rises. The sound barrier will be broken and the Voice of SHI will be heard very clearly in the hearts of all of Humankind. The hearts of humans will then be filled with tenderness, for all, through knowing God. Your Teacher says that tenderness goes beyond empathy; it eclipses compassion. It is a divine attribute and as the higher evolved level of heart consciousness develops, the old heart of the lower self will atrophy.

Your Teacher goes on to say, "The doctrine of 'The Fall from Grace' will be cast aside when the Great Event occurs due to the rise again of Direct Experience of SHI. The level of Direct Experience that will be gained will be because the haze that is at present over all that is Divine will be removed. Those who are prepared for the Ultimate Expression of Humans coming into being will be able to tolerate the Light of SHI at the level that is in Star Beings.

"The upgrading of the Human Being is the final part of the Divine Plan for the salvation of Humankind. It is to save humans from completely losing awareness of their Divine Nature. This happened in a previous experiment because after a while, many Human Beings used the powers that they had been given to achieve great things for themselves instead of great things for the Glory of God. Bountiful gifts will be given so that the progress of the Human Race can be maintained at a higher evolved spiritual level.

"The increase of the Divine Force in Human Beings will enable dimensions to be opened up to the current Civilization that they have had no awareness of. Information about The Light, which was sewn deep into the fabric of the soul, will come to the fore. Once the knowledge starts to be released, centuries of misunderstanding of The Profound will come to an end. Humankind will go forward singing the same song; appreciating each note and harmonizing with the melody in a way that has not been achieved for a very long time. This will be because God's Time will have come on Earth again."

Your Teacher says that as the magnificent fragrance of The Rose has enraptured you during the Initiation; the beauty of The Rose has enchanted you; the magnetism of The Rose has enthralled you, and your attunement to the energy of the God Chakra has taken you to a new level of wisdom, understanding and growth, your heart's mind will be able to assimilate what he is going to reveal to you. He tells you that the reason for the upgrade is so that the higher vibration of The Light of the World[1] can be fully reflected in all of Humankind.

The High Priest gently kisses your brow again and advises you that when you gaze with the enhanced beam of the light from your Third Eye Chakra, you will now be able to see fleet images of the processes of The Light. He says to let them flow unhindered and once you are accustomed to the finer, faster energy in your being, even more wondrous images of SHI will be revealed to you. The first image that you see is of your Teacher standing next to the Tree of Life. He raises his arms above his head and a gold ray from the Great Central Sun turns the Tree's trunk, branches, and leaves a lovely glowing gold colour. Some of the leaves start falling off of the Tree and you remember that St. John The Divine revealed that the leaves of the Tree were for the healing of the Nations.[2]

[1]Gospel of St. John 8:12, Jesus spoke to them saying, "I am The Light of the World."
[2]The Revelation of St. John The Divine 22:2

The High Priest informs you that one of the tasks of Human Light Bringers will be to gather and distribute the gold leaves of wisdom to help Nations prepare for the Great Shift. The image of the High Priest/High Priestess disappears and is replaced by a vision of The Rose in a gold garment. Instantly you become aware of the exquisite fragrance of The Rose and realize that you are back in the Inner, Inner Sanctum of the Sacred Heart Centre.

Archangel Metatron gives you a huge hug and congratulates you on all that you have achieved during the Initiation; for, he says, you have not only experienced what it is like to walk in God's Garden and go along the Arbour of The Rose; you have also felt the sensation of your heart on fire with the Love of SHI, as he had done during his lifetime as Enoch. Your Guardian informs you that your endurance and perseverance in completing all three grades of the Initiation have been highly praised and with that he gives you a scroll.

On the seal of the scroll is an image of an eagle. The Archangel tells you that the eagle is one of the guises of the Great Spirit of SHI. It signifies that the scroll was delivered by the Messenger of Great Spirit whose name is St. John The Divine. Your heart is filled with joy when you open the scroll, for it says:-

GUERDON OF GRACE

✳ ✳ ✳

In recognition of successfully completing all three grades of the Light Bringer Initiation,

.... (Your Name)

has been rewarded with the Grace that is bestowed upon all Light Bringers. The level of spiritual wealth that is received elicits awe and true humility. It is to be used wisely and always from the heart.

This certificate has been delivered to you with the profound Blessing and the Absolute Love of

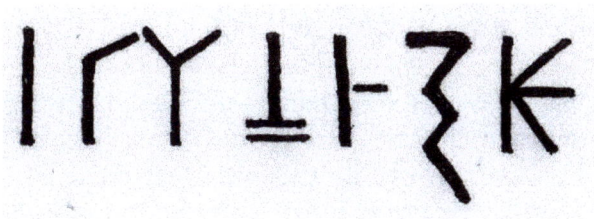

After you have thanked, with a deep feeling of gratitude and love, all who helped you obtain the Guerdon of Grace, Metatron tells you what your mission is going to be. It is to help other Human Beings prepare for the Great Event of the re-opening of the God Chakra. You will also be assisting Light Bringers who are already engaged in increasing the Flow of Light in the World in readiness for the New Dawn.

Your Guardian taps your Third Eye Chakra and a vision of The Rose in a red garment appears. You watch in amazement as you see the petals of The Rose scattered throughout the Cosmos. The Archangel explains that this insight not only illustrates the immeasurable amount of love that is in SHI's Heart; it also demonstrates the level of Divine Love that will be in the hearts of Humankind as a consequence of the Great Shift, for they will not only love those dwelling on Earth; they will also love all of Creation. He tells you that the purpose of the Ladder of Ascending Heart Consciousness is to gain a true sense of belonging to SHI's Extended Family which is vast.

Metatron goes on to say that after the Great Shift, the inhabitants of the 'Beacon of the Cosmos' will eventually become Light Bringers to those, elsewhere in the Cosmos, who will have not reached the level of spiritual development that Earth Beings will have gained by that time. This is because the thoughts that arose in human minds, before the Great Event, that did not always come from love will arise no more. Any darkness that was in them will be overcome by the level of the light that will be in their Heart Chakras. The pure light thoughts that will be emitted from humans will be due to a part of their brains becoming more crystalline.

Your Guide taps your Third Eye Chakra again and an image of The Rose in a white garment emerges. He says that it attracts souls who are in awe of the magnetism of The Rose. Once they are aware of The Name, through the Grace of God, powers are returned to them, which were closed down a long time ago. They will not be able to be misused and great things will be achieved for SHI.

When the Archangel taps your Third Eye Chakra for the third time, a vision of The Rose in a gold garment comes into view again. He informs you that it signifies that the armour that you have been provided with for your mission is the divine wisdom that comes from knowing the Name of SHI.

Metatron tells you that now that you have this level of awareness about SHI there is some more knowledge that he needs to pass over to you with regards to your appointment as a Light Bringer. It is, however, time for you to return to the Material Realm. Before you put the mantle of your physical being back on, he advises you to affirm, **I am powerfully protected by, and connected to, the Love and the Light of I-I-I mmmmmmm roo-oo-oo-oo-shhh-shhh-shhh inggg-inggg-inggg Ahhh, k-tahhh-ahhh-ahhh zer-er-er Ahhh, shoo-oo-oo-oo-shhh-shhh-shhh Ahhh, si-i-i sa-a-a L^ Ahhh, mw br rrr-rrr-rrr zzz Ahhh, fw^ zzz zer-er-er, i-i-i L^ ee-ee-ee shhh-shhh-shhh Ahhh, w-w-w j-j-j I-I-I Ahhh, wm dd-dd-dd der-er-er ree-ee-een Ahhh^ at all times; slowly return to the physical world; make sure that** you are completely grounded by feeling the floor of the room that you are in beneath your feet; wash your face and hands in cold water, and then drink a glass of cold water.

Once you are fully back in your temporary home what your Guardian wanted to convey to you flows into your heart's mind. It concerns the attributes that are essential regarding the effectiveness of a Human Light Bringer.

HUMILITY

If the ego takes over, the powers, which are granted by the Grace of God, can be taken away. The anguish of those whose powers have been removed can be profound.

MAGNETISM

The magnetism of The Rose has pierced your Heart Chakra. The white light that will be emitted from this energy centre will attract those who are ready to receive the knowledge that you have received about the Great Event, thereby helping you in your quest to achieve great things for God during your mission.

HOLINESS

There cannot be a more profound level of understanding of SHI unless you are holy. This is because God is holy. When the Great Shift occurs, the level of holiness that Human Beings once possessed will be returned because of the re-opening of the God Chakra.

UNDERSTANDING

The flames of the Great Spirit of SHI, in the Burning Rose Bush, burnt away what was no longer needed. It illuminated how the warmth of SHI's Cherishing can entail the removal of things that need to be replaced or renewed. This can be difficult to understand. God works in mysterious ways and only those who are ready to understand them are given the means to grasp why certain things happen. The purification that will occur, as a result of the Great Shift, will enable greater understanding of God's Works to arise in human hearts. This is because there will be the level of Ascended Heart Consciousness for them to be perceived in their true context. In the meantime, for each one that you share the knowledge that you have been given, a greater level of understanding about the Great Event will be granted to you.

REVERENCE

To know the Name of SHI, before the Great Shift, is a very precious gift to be given and it is to be "exalted above all blessing and praise." When it is expressed as a sacred mantra, with the utmost reverence, an exponential increase in spiritual growth can occur.

GUIDANCE

Growth

This section contains ways to continue increasing the level of spiritual growth that has been gained as a result of the Initiation.

THE NAME

You need to start by doing what is necessary, which is to express the Name of SHI with your inner voice, and your outer voice, at least once a day. To help you maintain the focus, keep a fresh rose, if possible, or a silk rose, on your meditation table. Whilst you are expressing The Name, gently rock your body slightly forwards and then backwards in the rhythm of a fairly fast heartbeat. Stop moving in this way when you sing the letters, **'zer',** and instead slowly rotate your head in a small anticlockwise circle. When you express the word **'der'**, slowly rotate your head in a small clockwise direction. The elongation of the letters of The Name, The Powers and The Mysteries is only a guide. If you persevere with singing them, in time the right level of elongation will come to you and what may have seemed impossible to master, will be achievable with ease. The abbreviations used in the explanation of the pronunciation of The Name, The Powers and The Mysteries are as follows, a/i means as in; s/l means sounds like, and r/w means rhymes with.

I-I-I mmmmmmm roo-oo-oo-oo-shhh-shhh-shhh inggg-inggg-inggg Ahhh

(I (s/l eye)- mmm (s/l humming)- roo (a/i root)- shhh-ing (a/i ring (the sound of 'g' is emphasized))- ahhh)

k-tahhh-ahhh-ahhh zer-er-er Ahhh

(k (a/i kite)- tahhh (r/w far)- zer (r/w her)- ahhh)

shoo-oo-oo-oo-shhh-shhh-shhh Ahhh

(sh-oo (a/i shoe)-shhh- ahhh)

si-i-i sa-a-a L^ Ahhh

(si (a/i sit)- sa (a/i sat)- L (a/i look (the sound of L is emphasized)- ahhh)

mw br rrr-rrr-rrr zzz Ahhh

(m (a/i make)- w (a/i wake)- br (a/i bright)- rrr- zzz-ahhh)

fw^ zzz zer-er-er Ahhh

(f (a/i fine)- w (a/i wine)- zzz- zer (r/w her)- ahhh)

i-i-i L^ ee-ee-ee shhh-shhh-shhh Ahhh

(i (a/i it)- L (a/i look (the sound of 'L' is emphasized))-ee (a/i free)- shhh- ahhh)

w-w-w j-j-j I-I-I Ahhh

(w (a/i wade)- j (a/i jade)- I (s/l eye)- ahhh)

wm dd-dd-dd der-er-er ree-ee-een Ahhh^

(w (a/i wake)- m (a/i make)- dd (d (a/i dove)-der (r/w her)-reen (r/w seen)- **Ahhh**)

THE POWERS

CLAIRVOYANCE

Dagerdu Ahhh

Dahhh-ahhh-ahhh ger-er-er du Ahhh

(dahhh (r/w far)- ger (r/w her)- du (a/i do)- ahhh)

CLAIRAUDIENCE

Weezonfat Ahhh

Wee-ee-ee zo-o-on fa-a-at Ahhh

(we- zon (r/w on)- fat (r/w hat ('t' is stressed))- ahhh)

CLAIRSENTIENCE

Buseenet Ahhh

Bu-u-u see-ee-ee ne-e-et Ahhh

(bu (r/w too)- see- net (r/w set ('t' is stressed))- ahhh)

CLAIRMONSTRANCE

Pagrodisvu Ahhh

Pahhh-ahhh-ahhh gro-o-o di-i-is vu-u-u Ahhh

(pahhh- gro (a/i grow)- dis (r/w hiss)- vu (r/w too)- ahhh)

CLAIRRESONANCE

Pepertan Ahhh
Pe-e-e per-er-er tay-ay-ayn Ahhh
(pe (a/i pet)- per- tan (r/w gain)- ahhh)

CLAIROBSERVANCE

Moleevu Ahhh
Mo-o-o lee-ee-ee vu-u-u Ahhh
(mo (s/l mow)- lee (r/w see)- vu (r/w too)- ahhh)

CLAIRCOGNISANCE

Paseeranusveech Ahhh
Pahhh-ahhh-ahhh see-ee-ee ra-a-a nu-u-us
vee-ee-eech Ahhh
(pahhh- see- ra (a/i ray)- nus (r/w bus)- vich (r/w beach)-
ahhh)

You may find it helpful to re-read the chapter called, 'God's Gifts,' regarding The Name and in the chapter called, 'God's Garden,' the section called, 'The Conservatory,' concerning The Powers and The Mysteries. Singing the names of The Powers and The Mysteries every day, as well as The Name, can help you to gain a higher level of awareness of them.

THE MYSTERIES

GOD'S GRACE

YImozemfaktor Ahhh
Y-Y-Y I-I-I mo-o-o ze-e-em fa-a-ak tor-or-or Ahhh
(y (a/i your)- I (s/l eye)- mo (s/l mow)- zem (r/w hem)-
fak (r/w back)- tor (a/i tor)- ahhh)

THE MAGNETISM OF THE ROSE

Isneemuspouvareen Ahhh
i-i-i s-s-s nee-ee-ee mu-u-us po oo-oo-oo vahhh-
ahhh-ahhh ree-ee-een Ahhh
(i (a/i it)- s (a/i seek)- nee (a/i knee)- mus (r/w bus)-
po (a/i post)- oo (a/i ooze)- vahhh (r/w car)- reen (r/w
seen)- ahhh)

THE RETURN

Husgerveenerbedeesem Ahhh
Hu-u-us ger-er-er vee-ee-ee ner-er-er
be-e-e dee-ee-ee se-e-e mmmm Ahhh
(hus (r/w bus)- ger (r/w her)- vee (r/w see)- ner
(r/w her)- be (a/i bed)- dee (a/i deep)- se (a/i set)-
m (s/l humming)- ahhh)

THE BURNING BUSH

Mozenbikdeela Ahhh

Mo-o-o ze-e-en bi-i-ik dee lahhh-ahhh-ahhh Ahhh

(mo (s/l mow)- zen- bik (r/w pick)- dee (a/i deep) la (r/w far)- ahhh)

GOD'S NAME

FeeveroL^tu Ahhh

Fee-ee-ee ver-er-er o-o-o L too-oo-oo Ahhh

(fee- ver (r/w her)- o (a/i only)- **L** (a/i look (the sound of '**L**' is emphasized))- too- ahhh)

The symbol ^ after **L** indicates that your arms should be raised above your head, with your hands in prayer position, as the letter is expressed, just as they are when this letter is sounded when The Name is sung. Whether you are singing The Name, or the name of the Mystery of God's Name, if you close your physical eyes when you raise your arms regarding this letter, as well as the other letters in The Name that have the ^ symbol next to them, you will, in time, see with your Third Eye gold light emerge as these letters are being sung.

CELESTITE CHAKRA GRID

Once you have read through the whole meditation on the Initiation, you may feel ready to experience Celestite crystals being put on the chakras as shown on the next page. A large white sheet should be placed over a duvet, or whatever you choose to lay on, so that you feel comfortable whilst you are lying on the floor. You will need to have someone with you to set out the crystals in the right places, as the ten Celestite crystals are put on the body, head and following chakras:-

a)   Heart Chakra
b)   Left Shoulder – Throat Chakra – Right Shoulder
c)   Left Ear and Right Ear
d)   Third Eye Chakra
e)   Crown Chakra
f)   Soul Chakra
g)   Stellar Gateway Transpersonal Chakra

Very small crystals should not be placed in your ears. Medium size crystals that can be taped across your ears are ideal. Doing this helps to bring about the quietness and serenity that is essential for a deeper level of meditation to be obtained. The crystals that are placed on both shoulders can also be taped. They are laid out in a straight line with the crystal on the Throat Chakra in the centre of the line. Besides being part of the arrowhead, the stones that are put on the shoulders reflect the ability to responsibly carry, and use wisely, the knowledge that is revealed to you whilst you are meditating.

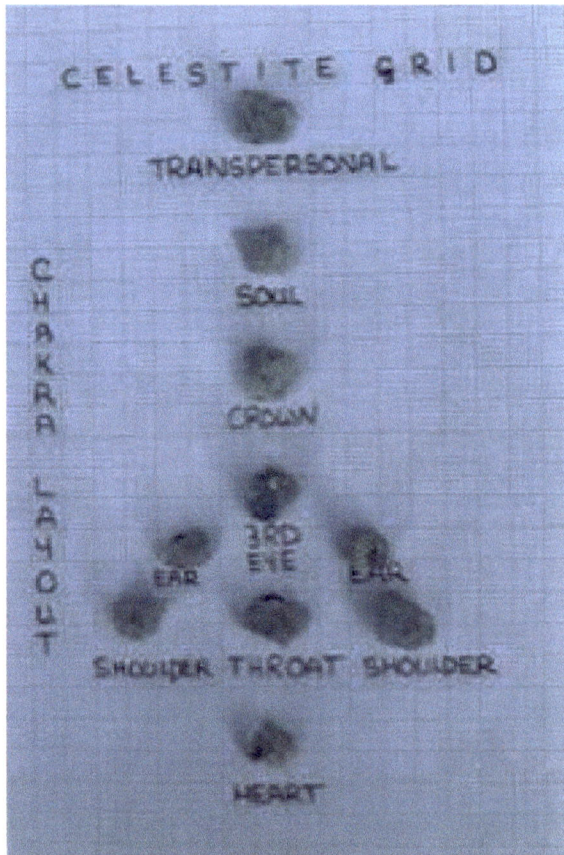

CELESTITE GRID

TRANSPERSONAL

SOUL

CROWN

CHAKRA LAYOUT

3RD EYE

EAR   EAR

SHOULDER THROAT SHOULDER

HEART

The Soul Chakra is approximately 6 inches above the top of your head and the Stellar Gateway Transpersonal Chakra is approximately 12 inches above the top of your head, hence the need for a large sheet.

After you have let your helper know that you are ready to state, with your inner voice, the intention for using the Celestite Chakra Layout, which is to obtain more knowledge about the God Chakra, **your helper should make sure that you are not in the Grid for longer than twenty minutes, and that they bring you back from the meditation very slowly and very gently. It is essential that mobile phones are turned off before the meditation starts and are not switched on until you are fully back to everyday awareness.**

CRYSTAL SKULL CAP

The Crystal Skull Cap, which was worn during Grade III of the Initiation, was described in the chapter called, 'God's Grace.' Its function was to help you attune to the Ultimate Expression of the Human Being. One way to ensure that your understanding of the Jewel of Consciousness/the Mysteries of Creation keeps on developing is to make your own Crystal Skull Cap. You will need to get the following items. They are available on Amazon.

10 Small Purple Silk Pouches that have a zip
2 x 7cm Hair Grips

The pouches are easy to sew together to make the Skull Cap. Alternatively, you could sew the pouches on to a lightweight cotton balaclava. Once you have made the cap, instead of holding a stone against or sticking crystals on to chakras such as the Third Eye Chakra; the Crown Chakra, or the Mouth of God/Medulla Chakra, in order to bring the energy in them into harmony with the frequency that the crystals are vibrating on that you are going to be working with; the stones can be placed in the Crystal Skull Cap. I received some fascinating information, which you will find in the section called, 'Gaia's Gifts,' when I put the following crystals in the Crystal Skull Cap that I had made:-

AGNITITE

The name Agnitite is derived from Agni, the Vedic god of fire. I hold this crystal when I am working with the goddess, Brigid, who is called, the Midwife. She is assisting with the birthing of greater understanding of the Fire of Spirit. The crystal is associated with the sensation of feeling that your heart is on fire with the Love of SHI.

ANANDALITE

Anandalite is also known as Aurora Quartz. It is associated with the expansion of consciousness via the kundalini's journey to its ultimate destination. The name of this stone is derived from the Sanskrit word, Ananda, which means Divine Bliss, and I certainly feel this each time I visit The Garden whilst I am holding this crystal.

APOPHYLLITE

Apophyllite has a gentle energy and is perfect for meditation and interdimensional travel. If this crystal is put in the Crystal Skull Cap pouch that is over the Third Eye Chakra it can assist in enhancing prophetic abilities. Placing the stone in the pouch that is over the Crown Chakra can help in the expansion of consciousness of the Angelic Realms.

ARAGONITE

This crystal, like Celestite, assists with communication with Angelic Beings whilst in the meditative state. Aragonite can enable access to past lives to be gained as well. Singing the name of the Clairobservance Power, Moleevu Ahhh, whilst holding this crystal, can enhance the knowledge that can be obtained about the spiritual evolvement that was achieved in your previous lifetimes.

AURALITE 23

This stone is also called, Canadian Amethyst and the Kindred Spirit Crystal. It can support contact with Higher Beings; help with assimilation of visions of future events and assist with the expansion of insight about them. It facilitates encountering human kindred spirits on a spiritual level as well as making it easier for there to be harmonious interactions within a Spiritual Group.

AZEZTULITE

White Azeztulite was the first variety of this 'new' crystal that was found. It is associated with assisting with attunement to higher chakras and information being obtained about the raising of Earth's and Humankind's vibration. Communication with High Angelic Beings called, 'The Azez,' who have been overseeing human's spiritual development for thousands of years, is possible whilst working with this crystal.

HERKIMER DIAMOND

The stone above is called a diamond because of its shape. These stones can assist when visiting higher dimensions by helping to clear fears about such journeys. Placing a Herkimer Diamond in a pouch in the Crystal Skull Cap next to a pouch that has a Moldavite stone in it can enhance cosmic consciousness.

MOLDAVITE

Moldavite's extraterrestrial origin is well known. It is a powerful Light Bringer and can accelerate spiritual growth. Attunement to the increase in vibration can be assisted by putting this stone into one of the pockets of the Crystal Skull Cap. It can also facilitate the journey up the Ladder of Ascending Heart Consciousness.

NIRVANA QUARTZ

The pink variety of Nirvana Quartz is particularly suited to assisting so that a more profound level of meditation is attained as it can facilitate attunement to pure consciousness. Through its support during the expansion of Heart Chakra consciousness, it can help to amplify the rapture associated with direct experience of The Divine.

SELENITE

Selenite's gentle energy is associated with helping to enhance attunement to the Divine Feminine. The crystal is named after the Greek Goddess of the Moon who was called Selene. Plates made out of Selenite are used to recharge other crystals as Selenite is linked to assisting in the raising of our vibration.

If you decide to fill all ten pouches with higher vibration crystals, whether they are Celestite Crystals or other high vibration crystals, **it is essential that you have worked with each crystal at least three times before you put them in the Crystal Skull Cap; you only wear the cap for a minute at a time to begin with; you very gradually build up to keeping the cap on for longer, and you ALWAYS HOLD YOUR HEMATITE STONE WHILST YOU ARE WEARING THE CAP.**

AMULET

In view of the acceleration of spiritual growth that is being undertaken in preparation for the New Dawn of The Light of the World, it is wise to wear an amulet to protect you. Following the description of the amulet in the chapter called, 'God's Grace,' I have set out the letters of The Name at the end of this book. They are the right size, once you have cut them out and folded them lengthwise, to fit into a gold-plated locket that is 3cm wide by 3cm long, or a signet ring with a secret compartment could be used. In place of the Tantermani Fiery stone, I have put a much smaller piece of Alexandrite in my locket than the one below.

Alexandrite is associated with the celestial joy that comes from experiencing the Absolute Love of The Divine whilst visiting the higher dimensions. It should be noted that what occurs whilst holding or wearing different crystals depends on which powers have been awakened in you.

Gaia's Gifts

≡<>≡

The revival of the knowledge, which was realized in ancient times, about the powers some of Gaia's Gifts possess is significant. In recent years, 'new' crystals, some of which have been hidden for thousands of years waiting to be discovered, have been found. They have included Light Bringer crystals that have knowledge stored in them that is relevant to the New Dawn of The Light on Earth and/or The Light of The World. You only have to hold certain ones up to a light source to witness the beauty of the light that is in them. Quite a few of the 'new' crystals have been added to the extensive stock of crystals that Keith maintains. They have either come from his suppliers or another source.

In the past, Keith conducted several crystal workshops with the renowned Crystal Expert, Judy Hall. Judy sadly passed away a few years ago. With the blessing of Judy's daughter, Jeni, Keith has been distributing crystals from Judy's large collection of stones throughout the World via his website, ksccrystals.com. Contained within the collection, there are 'new' crystals as well as umpteen kinds of other types of stones. Approximately seven months after my book called, CRYSTAL MYSTICISM, was published, I was very fortunate to be able to buy, from Keith, the Mani Stone that belonged to Judy. There is another stone called, Mani, but it is a different type of stone than Judy's Mani Stone; for the Tibetan Mantra, OM

MANI PADME HUM, is engraved on Judy's stone, as shown below: -

OM MANI PADME HUM was the first mantra that I quoted in CRYSTAL MYSTICSM. Judy's Mani Stone has a lovely vibe and it seemed as though it was auspicious that it came to me at that time because I was about to start writing CRYSTAL INITIATION.

You may recall that OM MANI PADME HUM means, 'the Jewel of Consciousness is in the Heart Chakra.' The luminosity of the 'many splendoured' jewel is pure. It is bright shining like the sun and the warmth that is emitted from it is the outpouring of the warmth of the expression of the Great Soul of Light Supreme's Love. The facet of the jewel that contains the image of The Rose reveals the incredible beauty of the jewel and the marvellous thing is that no matter how high up the Ladder of Ascending Heart Consciousness you go, there is always more to learn about the jewel.

The combination of the Great Mani mantra, which is linked to enhanced spiritual awareness; meditation, which is a potent force for spiritual growth, and high vibration crystals/stones that have been gathered because they are known to assist in the accumulation of spiritual wealth, can result in knowledge being brought to the surface that has been buried deep in the subconscious. In a similar way information can lay undiscovered, deep underground, for a very long time until a series of actions are taken that brings about a breakthrough. Whilst wearing the Crystal Skull Cap during meditation, I have recently been made aware that a major advance in the Palaeontology Field is on the horizon. A backbone will be found that has a fossil fused on it that had had an Extraterrestrial modus operandi. This will mean that the timeline that has been established, by humans, for the evolvement of life on Earth will need to be relinquished. It will lead to greater understanding being gained about Atlantis.

CRYSTAL INITIATION completes the trilogy of ATLANTIS: AS BELOW SO ABOVE, which contains information about Atlantis rising once more as well as revealing how I came to know SHI's Name; and CRYSTAL MYSTICISM, which brings into focus SHI's Name again and sheds light on the image of The Rose in the Inner, Inner Sanctum of the Sacred Heart Chakra. In every one of these books reference is made to Gaia's Gifts. This is because the crystals/stones that have a connection with the Higher World are helping us to prepare for the New Dawn of The Light of The World – the Great Event of the return of the whole of the Holy Self. This is so that a time that is similar to the Golden Age of Atlantis can arise.

All that is left for me to do now is to give you a big hug and say, "Goodbye" .... or is it?

Goodbye?

≡<>≡

Although the meditation on the Initiation has come to an end, the connections that have been made will carry on.

Cherished Soul Companion, there are no goodbyes in the World of Light. This is because it operates on God's Time, which is the Eternal Now, and you are forever held in its sway.

I do, however, want to convey to you my heartfelt wish for you to fare-well. May your attunement to high vibration crystals continue to grow now that you are au fait with the benefits of the crystal grid's array; may the thought of visiting higher dimensions of The Light no longer fill you with dismay and through God's Grace, may more facets of the Jewel of Consciousness in the Heart Chakra be opened up to you; for that is one of the wonderful blessings that can arise from singing SHI's Name The Cherishing way.

With warm and tender love, I say,
"Peace be with you,
NAMESTE."

Lindsey Elizabeth Day

I m roo shhh ing Ahhh k-tah zer Ahhh
shooshhh Ahhh si sa L Ahhh mw br r z Ahhh
fw z zer Ahhh i L ee shhh Ahhh w j I Ahhh
wm dd der reen Ahhh

www.ingramcontent.com/pod-product-compliance
Lightning Source LLC
LaVergne TN
LVHW010307070426
835513LV00022B/2413